Are you a Mum, Wife or
a little help on balancing
demands?

Within this book, you will take away some incredibly simple systems and working formats from a successful Business Woman, Mum and Wife.

Get ready to be inspired - I think this book is definitely for you!

Gail

Introduction

Written by Rosie

age 6½

"This book has been written by my mum.

My mum says... this book is for anyone that wants to make money working from home and building a business like she does.

She likes to share and care and help everyone. My mum always reminds us that giving is a good thing to do and she often gives me lots of huggles even when she's working!

She says that lots of other mummy's out there would love to spend more time with their family like she does.

So my mummy is sharing her gifts of knowledge and experience with you in this book. So that your children can get more huggles   Rosie
from you too."

My mum says...

"Running a business from home is like

Child's Play!"

Mum's The Word!

*"My Mum-
She's the
Business!"*

Written by my Mum
and Business Woman
Gail Reynolds

Published by
Filament Publishing Ltd
16, Croydon Road, Waddon,
Croydon, Surrey CR0 4PA
+44 (0)20 8688 2598
www.filamentpublishing.com

ISBN 978-1-905493-90-6

Printed by Berforts Group - Stevenage and Hastings

Find out more about Gail Reynolds on
www.gailreynolds.co.uk

Contents

Gail and family

Mum to 3 kids: Rosie, Libby and Ashleigh

A woman in business since 2002

Wife and best friend to Brian since 2003

A Foreword is forewarned

I am Gail Reynolds - a mum, wife, Network Marketer and business woman in the UK.

I hope you enjoyed the introduction from my little Rosie. You will hear more from her as you delve into this book.

To follow are a few facts you will probably need to know about me to gain some forward thinking of how I can help you in some way in your business. In this book I will share with you some simple ideas and simple techniques that will enhance your personal life as well as your home life and business.

As I said I am a Network Marketer, MLM'er, Direct Seller, Party Planner and business owner, and have been since 2002. I love what I do and simply want to share my success with you.

From One woman
to another

From One mum to
another

From One business owner
to another

A note about me

I left school at age 15 with no qualifications; I worked in factories and shops until I was 18. At the grand old age of 18 I was pregnant. I left home, moved in with my boyfriend, had my baby boy and went onto benefits.

At age 25 I was left holding a second baby (Libby); by now Ashleigh was coming up to 8 years old and Libby was 6 weeks old. I now had two children from two different dads, had never married and lived in a flat on a council estate.

I had no experience in the business world and certainly no knowledge of how to sell, but here I am writing this book to show you just how you can secure a beautiful future for you and your family like I have.

Now I can almost run my business with my eyes shut!

"This driving thing is
so easy I can do it with
my eyes shut!"

Rosie

Throughout the book I will refer to the industry I work within as my network or my business purely because it helps you the reader have an easy reading experience without the jargon! It will also help you understand that no matter what line of work you are in, whether you are a mum like me or not in any business or network, you too can learn from the ideas I am going to give you.

The way my network and business works is pretty simple. I sell products to my personal customers and earn a commission based on their total order value. The system was pretty simple to follow and once I had secured the fact I could easily find customers to sell to, the rest of my job was easy. It was like baking a cake; so long as I had the correct ingredients, the team size would raise in figures and sales. Following that my earnings would raise too, giving me the perfect recipe to continually grow and expand my business.

Teamwork divides the task
and multiplies the success

Within the industry I am known as a Team Leader or Sales Leader. I recruit people to do the same as I do, find customers, take care of their customers and earn from their customers' orders. In duplicating what works over the years I have managed to help thousands of women (and a few men) all earn their own income from their own sales and they have all become independent business women in their own rights.

I basically manage my team of representatives and team leaders by giving total support, knowledge and guidance on how to earn more money for themselves and their families. Some of those women (of which the majority of my team are) go on to become leaders and recruiters like me.

So it's easy really. I endeavour to:
• Learn new and simple techniques
• Share them with my team
• Expand mine and their income
• Earning even more money for both themselves and their families

Everyone that is within the network will be achieving all of this from what is based on a "Work from Home Business".

My mum says...

"Working for yourself gives
you time for moments like this"

A note about the team

My team of customers, representatives and team leaders have been one of the fastest growing teams within my company's Network since we won 'The Team of the Year Award' in 2008.

My team's growth of:
- Sales
- Representatives
- Team Leaders and
- Income

have all increased every year since I began business in 2002.

I believe the fact that I became a mother for the third time during my business has given me more versatility; more reason and more of a willingness to learn and make my family unit never have wants or needs like I had when I was growing up as a child.

I gave birth to Rosie in 2005 smack bang in the middle of my business. I had to go back to basics and make sure my time was spent well. Yet the year she was born the business still had a growth in all areas.

"This is me, Rosie.
I met and kissed Daisy the
Dolphin with my mummy,
daddy, Ashleigh and Libby.
This is one of my most
favourite times"

My earnings have increased year on year since the day I began my business, and in 2010 my team turned over £5.5 million in sales and now in 2011 we are nearing the £6.2 million mark.

In 2010 I was able to take all my family to swim with dolphins and experience something beyond words. Just seeing and feeling such pride like I felt that holiday was worth every minute in business, every night away from home and even every risk I took to build the security of my business.

I highly suspect swimming with dolphins is something that millions of women only dream they could do with their families too. Well I dare you to believe that you can!

"This is my mummy & daddy winning
The Team of the Year Award. I am
very proud of them"
                    Rosie

A note about my Network

My Networking Business website www.gailsreps.co.uk gives vital information to anyone that wants to know more about me as a mum, housewife and more importantly as a business woman.

By 2011 me and my hubby Brian will have had over 21 years of combined knowledge in the world of Business, working from home, Network Marketing, Direct Selling and MLM.

This book is written to give you the simple business processes we use in our network every day.

This book is a gift from me. It is to offer you and other businesses an insight to how a woman can become as successful as anyone else in business and network marketing today.

If anything you have read so far resonates with you and your situation right now then this book is definitely for you.

Please keep an open mind into what you are about to read. Although this book is based on a business success plan for Multi Level Marketing, Direct Selling and Network Marketing, I know the same techniques and ways of thinking can enhance any woman's business today, whatever your business may be.

My mum says...

"Running a business of your own isn't SO scary"

Believe in Belief

Money can buy all kinds of things.

But what I want to share with you is how to buy your desires, your dreams, and your wealth in happiness and your financial freedom.

Our simple business systems helped us to buy ours. I can only show you how to become wealthy from within, so whatever you are looking for whether it's an harmonious family life or a BIG beautiful home or even a holiday abroad each year, you decide what your wealth is and I will help all I can to make sure you achieve it.

Using a belief system to success is a great philosophy to have.

I believe that the road to becoming successful is there for any woman to take; they just have to decide on what road they want to take.

My mum says...
"Wealth is

within you,

not the money

in the bank"

The hardest thing to learn is the self belief system.

Many people rely upon others to help them feel good about themselves.

To be told things like;

"You are great at what you do."

Or maybe;

"I know you can do it."

Any comments like these will make you feel good and help you continue and remain focused on your goal ahead.

So here is where your 1st lesson begins..... We all know that kind and encouraging words like the above can literally change our moods, make our day and have us feeling good on the inside.

So why aren't you doing it for yourselves, every single day? I would like to show you the way to your belief system.

Once upon a time

Here is a little story for you. (It isn't true, but just imagine the effects if it were)

Rosie comes home from a day at school and she says,

"Mummy, Mummy,
I painted a picture for you at school
today! Do you like it?"

In reply to Rosie, I say "Oh Rosie. I don't wear ponytails and our garden has no flowers! Why have you got yellow hair? You have brown hair!"

Do you really think this would happen?

No, it simply wouldn't do, would it?

I have always told my children that their drawings are the most colourful and beautiful pictures I have ever seen, and I simply can't wait to get it up on the fridge for everyone to see. I have always lovingly instilled a belief system that Rosie and my other children have always been wonderful artists with an imagination beyond words. With doing this, I have created a simple belief system into them and their capabilities and abilities. So here is how to use the same technique but for yourself.

Here is what I do as part of my belief system. I tell myself every day "I can do that". It has always been a funny joke between me and my mother-in-law Lorraine that whenever we see or hear something new on the TV or radio or read it in the newspapers, Lorraine would say "Gail can do that!" in chorus with me saying "I can do that!".

So here is a good way for you to start your belief techniques. Go to a mirror; go on.... go to a mirror....

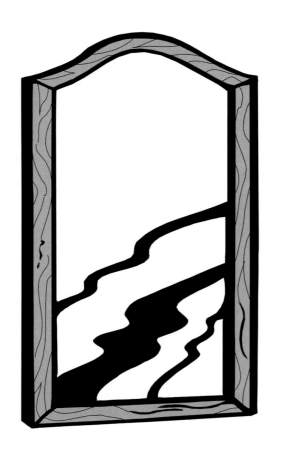

Look at yourself

and say out loud

*"I look great, I feel great,
and I can do anything"*

The "Mirror Technique" is a great way to build a business or a network. It's about painting a picture of you and your business and believing in the finished piece of art.

Building a business will involve talking to people, letting them know about you and your great new business and all its opportunities - products and services it has to offer them. It's about your finished painting.

But, how can you "Sell your colourful picture (your business)" if you have no self belief or feelings of wonderment about it to begin with?

Every day you need to know you can do anything. So by following the "Mirror Technique" you will see just how easy it becomes to paint a beautiful and colourful picture for yourself and for others to believe in.

Building your business is just like the child that paints a picture. Build it with love, passion and the knowledge that it is the best that you can make it. And before you offer your business opportunities and products or services to everyone you meet, repeat this simple sentence.

"I look great, I feel great, and I can do anything"

Once you master this simple technique you will have the power to believe in yourself and paint your own beautiful pictures. Then you can easily and confidently welcome others into your Network and your business.

Teamwork is essential for you to grow now. Your enthusiasm is the core of your business and its growth.

Growing a successful team is about painting the picture and following through. Keep your outlook positive, fun and achievable.

Don't ever be negative, dismissive or argumentative within your own team or business. Always encourage, motivate and incentivise those around you.

I have seen and heard many many team leaders and managers become angry, upset and annoyed at fellow team members because they haven't behaved or worked the way they wanted them too.

The only outcome I have ever seen with this is a breakdown in communication. The easy and only way to avoid this is to always remember the "Mirror Technique" and communicate with your team as if you were staring in that mirror.

REMEMBER:

Look at yourself
and say out loud

*"I look great,
I feel great,
and I can
do anything"*

Remind yourself that without feeling good about you it is impossible to; help - encourage - motivate and make others feel good too.

Whilst in your network marketing journey you will be up against hundreds of No's and some negative behaviour from others.

There are simple ways to deal with "The No's" and I would like to share them with you now.

In most industries and businesses we have to suffer with the constant rejections of;

"No thank you, I don't need your service, your product or your opportunity"

So, here we are at the most crucial part of your success in anything you set your mind too.

How many "No's" do you think the people at the top got whilst making their way there? Tens, hundreds, even thousands. But remember for all those "No's" they endured, there also came a few more "Yes's" too.

Small Blessings

Dear Lord, it's such a hectic day

With little time to stop and pray

For life's been anything but calm

Since You called on me to be a mom

Running errands, matching socks

Building dreams with building blocks

Cooking, cleaning, and finding shoes

And other stuff that children lose

Getting lids on bottled bugs

Wiping tears and giving hugs

A stack of last week's mail to read

So where's the quiet time I need?

Yet when I steal a minute, Lord

Just at the sink or ironing board

To ask the blessings of Your grace

I see then, in my small one's face

That you have blessed me

All the while

And I stop to kiss

That precious smile

Colonel Sanders

(1890 -1980)

At the age of 66
he created the
Kentucky Fried Chicken
fast food chain

Colonel Sanders was not born a rich man. His family background consisted of a divorced mother that remarried a man that beat the colonel from a young age. Sanders ran away from home and joined the United States army falsifying his age at 16.

At the age of 40, Sanders cooked chicken dishes and other meals for people who stopped at his service station in Corbin, Kentucky. Since he did not have a restaurant, he served customers in his adjacent living quarters.

When the Colonel reached 65 years of age, Sanders' store failed due to the new Interstate 75 reducing his restaurant's customer traffic. He took just $105 from his first Social Security cheque and began visiting potential franchisees.

My mum says...
"Don't monkey around,
just do it!"

At the age of 65, this man was not yet ready to give up. Although Colonel Sanders accumulated over 1000 No's for his secret KFC Recipe, he continued to approach potential investors. Then entered Mr David Thomas, the founder of Wendy's fast food chain. David managed to help the Colonel turn around the then failing KFC restaurant to enable him to sell the business. In 1964, the Colonel received $2 million for selling the KFC restaurant to a partnership of Kentucky businessmen.

So....are you a Colonel of your business?

I know I am. Like Colonel Sanders I know I have had my fair share of "No's" and I believe these are what have made me stronger and set me aside from other Network Marketers, Direct Sellers and MLM'ers in this industry.

All my hopes and my dreams were resting on all the "No's". But despite all of them, I am still here, I still believe I can make it to the top and I can achieve whatever I set my mind too.

Through my thousands of "No's" I grew stronger, more determined and much more successful. I have always had a strong belief that if I have enough passion, enthusiasm and determination within me then anything is possible.

My mum says...
"You too can be a
roaring success if you
just follow a simple system"

Keep in mind that you can't preach it if you don't do it! Simple!

There is a system for everyone no matter what their dream, desire, goal or target. So let's get down to basics.

Within your business, company and industry there will be:

- Basic structures to follow
- Basic business plans to follow
- Basic training to follow

But, what you do further to those basics is what sets you aside from the rest. Take what you know for sure and build on it. Be at the forefront of your business leading the way, proving to yourself that you are a worthy leader and business owner. Show that you are able to lead your team to their triumphs and desires. By them simply shadowing and duplicating you and your efforts, your team will also be a roaring success.

Teaching others your successes is the only way forward in any business.

My mum says...

"If you just trust in me, I can teach
you just how easy this
maths is"

Work and Life
Gratitude to guide you

There are many things in our lives that seem like meaningless daily chores and grinds. What if I could teach you how to see these as the most gratifying accomplishments you achieve daily and give yourself no recognition for? Let me try to explain.

Children

My mum says...

"Family time is the most
important time of the day"

We feed them, we dress them, we nurture them, we guide them and we provide them with unconditional love. Without you those children would be lost souls with no one to follow. They would have no one to look up to and no one to keep them warm and safe.

So from one mum to another I congratulate you.
Here is a heartfelt well done.

You truly are a magnificent parent.

"God could not
be everywhere
and therefore
he made
mothers"

A Jewish Proverb

Family & Friends

We comfort them when they are in need of a shoulder to cry on.

We visit them when they need help and advice.

We help them in their hour of need and we show them unconditional love and compassion.

We share their secrets, desires and their dreams.

Without you as a sister or maybe their daughter, their aunt or their cousin, or indeed their mother or friend, where would they be?

You are a great family member and an amazing friend and yet you don't seem to see or value your worth to your friends and family often enough.

My mum says...
"Friends & Family
are like quilts,
they never lose
their warmth"

Here is a simple exercise

How about you stop for a moment (yes, right now) and think about your friends and family members. Feel the gratitude for what you have and stop focusing on what you don't have.

You just need to open your eyes to what you achieve every day, look at exactly what you do have in your personal lives, and give thanks and gratitude for the simplest of your life's little treasures.

It was the lack of my friends' and family's love and support that got me to where I am today. I didn't realise the devastating effect it would have on me by moving home. It meant that I had lost that immediate connection with loved ones, and the support system was simply too far away. The situation made me take action to change the way things were.

So there I was, new to the area and completely without friends.

Although my daughter Libby and son Ashleigh were at school I was finding it hard to make friends with the mums and neighbours. After 3 months I was getting really depressed thinking of the friends I was missing back home.

"When my mummy is sad,
then I feel sad too"

So I took action

I looked in the local paper for another job (I was already working part time for 20 hours a week) but I was becoming desperate for friendships.

There before my very eyes in the "Situations Vacant" pages was the thing I had been desperately looking for.

> Meet New People & Earn Extra Cash
>
> CALL ME TODAY

It was perfect.

Within 48hrs of seeing the advertisement I was a representative for a Direct Selling company. I was confident I would be able to talk to the mums at the school gates now. This was going to be a great opportunity to show them all my products. More importantly though, I knew it was my opportunity to make some connections and start building friendships.

I wasn't wrong. Within less than a week, I knew the entire network of mums within Libby's year group. I was on first name terms with most of them and standing in the school playground wasn't so lonely anymore.

"When my mummy is happy,
then I feel happy too"

My loneliness wasn't an issue any longer.

I had taken ACTION.

I had found myself a solution to my problems.

Within my new role as a representative I quickly realised how many other representatives were in my local area too. My first goal was to make sure that any customers out there knew it was me they needed to come to for a friendly and professional service. So I set about promoting myself.

I am by nature a pretty happy person anyway. I am hard working and very creative too.

I am also widely known for my ability to share and care. (Rosie loves the Share and Care motto we use in our home) A great tip is to use the Sharing and Caring motto throughout your business and your lifestyle too.

From the bus drivers and postmen in the mornings to the lady that served you in the supermarket today. Sharing your appreciation for their service and showing you care about them is an amazing way to keep you focused on what you want from others too.

My mum says...

"Learners are Earners and Leaders are Readers"

I suppose when I began my business many years ago I started with a smart attitude. I became a student within the Network Marketing Industry.

I also figured that working with a cosmetics company was going to be pretty easy too.

I loved the products myself, so I knew it wasn't going to be at all difficult for me to find customers.

Since my early days, I have read many books, and watched and listened to many DVDs and CDs. I have learnt a wealth of knowledge from these and I like to think that "Learners are Earners" and "Leaders are Readers".

Today I liken myself to a sponge. I soak up as much information (as a sponge would soak up water) as possible. Then I use, apply and train others on what I have learnt. I strive to continually become better at what I do and what we do as a team of Network Marketers.

I like to learn new concepts and ideas. Taking tips, ideas and knowledge from others that are already at the top of their professions and industries is the smart thing to do.

From party planners to hairdressers and from other Multi Level Marketers to the owners of the fruit and vegetable shop down the road. Each business owner has their unique ideas and if you take the time to listen to others you may learn a thing or two along the way.

Remember this doesn't necessarily mean other Network Marketers. I have learnt that all people have created their own wealth from what they described as their,

"Desire & dream to make it BIG"

They didn't know how they were going to make it big, they just knew they were, no matter what.

If you haven't picked up a book for a while, or had a little chat with the local shop owner, then maybe you could do it today?

Maybe you pass the sweetie shop on the way back from school pick-up?
Pop in...
Get a lollipop for you and your little one and take some time to chat to the owner of the shop.

Ask them

"How are you today and how's business?"

Imagine the possibilities!

You may find yourself achieving some insightful business ideas from this one simple step. And don't forget the best bit - you made someone feel worthwhile today and possibly made them smile.

Why not make it your mission today to go to the library? (it's free there!) You can sit together with your little ones and read a fairytale and on your way out pick up a book that may give you ideas to help you grow your business for the better. Ask the librarian for their books about entrepreneurs or maybe some self help books. Think of the famous people you already know about or see on the TV and read their inspirational stories. Lord Sugar's autobiography is an inspiring read, and one of my personal favourites.

I promise you will be amazed at what you learn from the beginnings of these wealthy people. Their backgrounds and their lifestyles were much like yours and mine. But, they had a dream, they got told "No" but they also got told "Yes" and look where they are now.

Together
Everyone
Achieves
More

Your Team

Most businesses will be built around a team. So let's take a look at what your team's psychology looks like.

Are your team of representatives, party planners, distributors and leaders upbeat and ready for anything?

Or are they a little lethargic, slow and uncertain?

To begin you will need to talk to your team, one on one to start with, and then as a group.

Find a common goal from all of them; this is normally of a monetary value or status level within the business. Then focus on that goal.

Make your team united; together you will make an army of networkers to be reckoned with.

"A team that works together grows together"

I found that the easy way to create team spirit and a family unit within your business is to ask exactly what they want from you as their Team Leader. It's ok to know what you want from the team but do they know exactly what you want from them and is it what they want from their business?

We all have different desires and we all set different goals for ourselves.

My personal goal is to eventually own my own million pound home with a swimming pool for the kids. To have the family over and have BBQs in the summer and house parties in the winter. But that isn't going to be what my team members want; they may desire something simpler. Maybe they need a new washing machine, a holiday or enough money to be able to quit their other jobs?

By asking them what they want, you can secure a goal that suits everyone and gives everyone a place within the team.

Once you have decided what type of team you have and what their psychology as a whole is, then let's see if it could do with changing.

A slow and uncertain team is easier to mould. You can nurture, encourage and help grow their dreams into wealth and success. Just show them that you believe in them. You know they can do it; you will lead them from the front and navigate them to their desires and dreams. Let your team know that you will be their navigator to their dreams.

Always remain positive and become an avid listener to your team. If you have a team member that 'runs' at 100 miles an hour, then run with them, but more importantly get them to talk about their goals too.

I have been known to have this type of psychology and to be this type of person. It isn't always a great way to move forward. I have learnt to stop for a moment, reflect on what my goals are and maybe change gear and slow down.

Sometimes all it takes is to talk it through and find out what it is I actually want to achieve. I then have to sit back, think, write down and discuss my goal, control my passion, find out what end results I am after and then put my foot to the pedal again!

Many of my team members are the complete opposite to me. They sit, they think, they write it out and then think a little more. They also do a lot of research into their new project, idea, system or incentive so as to achieve the best results. Their actions show that their psychology is the total opposite to mine.

Both have extremely different styles and thought processes, but both are an asset to your individual businesses.

So.....
- Talk to your team
- Find out their dreams
- Discuss yours too

Now work together on them and turn your team into "A Dynamic Team".

Think BIG

Now I want you to look at your team and tell me is it 10 people strong or 1010? No matter what your team size, I am going to show you how to double, triple and even quadruple your figures by the end of the year.

"How do these words make you feel?"

TRUST

RELIABLE

ADVISOR

CREATIVE

FRIEND

TALKER

LISTENER

PRESENTER

PREPARED

SELF AWARE

FOCUSED

ENTHUSIASTIC

PASSIONATE

HELPFUL

REPUTABLE

DEDICATED

ENTREPRENEURIAL

There are hundreds more words I could have popped onto my list but I thought I would simply get to the point.

My team grows overnight. How?

It grows overnight because every day I do something for someone somewhere on and off my team and within the business environment.

If I can I want to take you back to the year 2002. There I was just beginning to grow my Networking Empire and business. I had just 5 new representatives that I went out and found that week all by myself.

I was buzzing. Here I was with 5 brand new representatives relying on me for most, if not all of the list I just wrote and more.

I both needed and wanted to make them proud of me and make them feel as good as I did now they were part of my team.

So I set about building my business around my personality.

I thought about what it was I could "Sell" about myself. It wasn't going to be my knowledge and experience in the business because I didn't have any yet. So I simply had to sell myself in order for other women to join my team, but more importantly stay with me and my team. So, what was I good at and what could I sell that was great about me?

I had a brainwave there and then. I was always good at talking, especially if I was passionate about the subject. I mean I could talk the hind legs of a donkey if you wanted to know about kids, organising my time and being a great enthusiast for life in general. So there it was. I had a great enthusiasm about me that even strangers would comment on when they first met me.

So, I would basically sell my enthusiasm to everyone I met. I would simply talk to them about my new business venture and the opportunities, products and services me and my team had to offer them.

I would like to share a story with you about a woman that I once met that owns a "Nail Salon".

It was school pick-up time and I had noticed the shop window a few times on my daily run.

It was a pretty nail salon and I could do with a little pampering time for myself so I noted the name of the salon and carried on with my daily chores. Once the kids were in bed, I sat down at my computer and Googled the salon. Website not found....

It was another 6 months or so before I thought about the salon again and the pampering time I so deserved. So this time, whilst passing the salon, I stopped my car, jotted down the number and went on my merry way.

A few weeks later I remembered the salon and decided to call. Amazingly a whole year had passed since my first thought of calling and having my nails done.

When I finally called, a very pleasant girl answered the phone and we booked an appointment for the following week.

I hadn't pampered myself in a while so I was really looking forward to the morning in the salon. When I arrived I was greeted by a lovely young receptionist that seemed a little nervous but nonetheless very friendly. She made me coffee and the owner walked in and greeted me.

Now, I am not much of a girly girl, but I do know how these things work. I am the customer and I am paying you for a service. Whether I walk into your shop with jeans and a t-shirt or a Dolce & Gabbana dress (I had to look that up by the way) you as the person offering the service should treat me with the same respect whatever I am wearing.

This unashamedly wasn't the case for this young business woman.

I felt the "Look" and her laser eyes checking out my shoes, clothes, coat, handbag and even the glasses I wore. I was just a "Joe Bloggs" of the street and she wasn't impressed.

We began chatting with a few pleasantries about the weather and such like and soon we began to discuss her business. She felt that she had slowed down on her regular and repeat customers and really couldn't understand why. After all she had got a little bit of a windfall and had enough money to redecorate her salon and got some fancy wallpaper hung on the walls. She also invested in some higher end of the market products to sell to her customers.

But, alas, new customers would come but not revisit and old customers had began to fall back too.

She had a note of despair in her voice but still a judgemental look on her face when she caught a glimpse of my non Dior or Chanel purse when I went to pay her for her services.

I had a choice - try to help her with her predicament or leave her to continue with her thoughts and woes. But, my chance to speak was abruptly taken away when she continued to moan on about how bad business was for her at the moment.

So "Why was it easy for her to find new customers but not keep them?" And "Why do you think she was losing her old and once loyal customers too?"

My mum says...

"No matter how much you succeed in business, your feet should always remain firmly on the ground"

Here is what I felt after just 1 hour with her.

She once had a friendly service that women could feel good about using. They would treat themselves without feeling too much of a pinch on the purse strings and come away feeling a little bit better about themselves.

She once made them feel comfortable about visiting her salon and they enjoyed their 45 minutes to an hour in this sanctuary of blissful pampering.

She once had a thriving customer base of which she had very loyal and repeat customers yet with her "Changes" to the salon came "Changes" to her too.

I felt the lady had one of two choices to have made with her business.

Leave it as it was and use the money to build a website for more and more people to find her. Or make the physical change to her salon but keep the same personality!

"People Buy from People"

I have found that often with success people change, and often with those changes comes things like conceitedness, rudeness and sometimes the "Complete know it all" attitude. None of which are attractive within women whatever their profession.

This lady had gone out of her way to make her customers feel uncomfortable because they didn't match up to her new standards. Her attitude had changed along with her wallpaper and her new products. This meant that her customers felt the changes too and so did I!

It is a lesson I have learnt and will always keep with me.

I know what I would have done to expand and help that business thrive but it wasn't for me to tell her. She was a talker and certainly not a listener. So I had my nails beautifully decorated and I went on my merry way. And no - I didn't go back!

But what I took from that visit was worth its weight in gold.

"Always be true to yourself"

Whatever you achieve and whatever your successes are, always remember who you are and where you have come from.

Thinking **BIG** comes with some unwritten rules to follow. Remain focused on your customer at all times and keep up with the changes that will benefit your niche market. Not the mass market. Customers should always remain at the forefront of your business.

To continue my story about my 5 new team members, I decided I was going to always be positive, encouraging and ready to help with whatever I could.

I went out with them to find customers, I helped them with their queries, and I developed them into successful recruits, representatives and distributors. I believe I managed to do this because I developed the following amongst them:

- I believed in them
- I shared every new idea I had with them
- I sent newsletters
- Set incentives
- Rewarded my top earners with gifts
- Certificates were sent in the post
- One on one visits remain a core part of my business

- Training
- Duplication
- Systems

I have found over the years that my ability to learn new techniques is a great skill and worth developing. I believe working on this particular skill was something that was going to help all parts of my business and it has done so ever since.

Now in 2011, with over 2500 people on my team I still do the same, but I have an army of over 220 team leaders that have put the same systems in place and we build our teams daily, therefore growing overnight is exactly what we do. No matter what your team size today, we all started somewhere.

Think BIG!

And today could be the first day of your true business success and potential.

Remembering your own goals are extremely important in your success. What was it you became a Network Marketer for and why did you start this business in the first place?

Ask yourself:

- "Why did you think starting your own business was a good idea?"

- "Is Direct Selling and MLM really what you thought it was going to be?"

- "What do you really want from this business?"

Maybe your answers will include some or even all of the following:

- Financial freedom

- A better quality of life

- Quality family time

- Money maybe?

- To offer a great service

- To follow your passion

The list is endless, so make sure you don't forget why you are in this business. Always remember your "Why's". It's important to remember your Why's especially if you are having a bad day. I still have them myself, but it only takes a glass of wine and a box of chocolates to help me remember why I started this business many years ago.

I always find that the next day it's crystal clear why I do this job - my family, my freedom and my quality of life are immense.

"I love it when my mummy takes me to the beach after school"

The Navigator of Dreams

To become a Navigator of Dreams you need to know a few things about the person that has set the dream or goal. Pick a team member. One you feel you could help the most, one with commitment, passion and desire, and talk to them about what it is they really want.

Begin to build a relationship with them and let them know that you believe in them and what they aspire to be.

Create a goal together, begin by writing everything down. (A top tip is to make sure they do the writing, it is their goal after all and you are just the navigator!)

You can see what's coming and you can help direct them in for landing but you can't fly the aeroplane for them (let them run their own business). Your navigation skills should lead them into a successful landing and a thriving business.

So, what are their personal targets, their goals, their desired ending to the task ahead?

My mum says...
"Think of yourself as
Air Traffic Control"

Maybe they dream of having:

- A new state of the art washing machine
- A brand new car
- A new luxurious home
- A new carpet for the baby's room

Let's consider the goal of the mum that wants a new carpet for the baby's room. Here is a way of creating that goal and navigating her through it to achieve the desired target.

The carpet for the baby's room

Ok, here is what you need to do:

Call your team member and arrange a time to visit. Find out the following personal details about her and her goal.

What's the baby's name? Remember it!

What colour carpet does she want?

What style?

The chosen pink colour looks so pretty
against her baby girl's cot and blankets

How much time does she have to achieve her goal?

Once you have gathered the information needed, find out the cost of the carpet by taking your team member to a carpet store. Ask for a sample of the carpet she wants and take it home. Now place it at the foot of her baby's cot so she can see it every night and every morning when the baby wakes up.

This is a great technique that will be a constant reminder of her goal and what actions she needs to take to achieve it. Now help her set a personal goal to buy her baby's new carpet.

The reminder of having the carpet at the foot of the baby's cot is a very powerful one.

The chosen pink colour looks so pretty against her baby girl's cot and blankets.

When she stands on the carpet to pick up her baby from her cot, she will feel the warmth and the quality of the carpet between her toes, a goal well worth working for!

She can imagine her little baby girl playing on the warm carpet in a couple of month's time. Inside her, she feels that she will achieve her goal and make it a reality. She now has a vision of her dreams and goals, and a very powerful one too.

Before you set the goal, remember you must:

Work through her time scales and how much commitment she is willing to put into achieving this goal.

Once the goal is set, you must now leave your team member to get on with the task and goal ahead. That is not to say you don't call, motivate and encourage her along the way. Everyone knows that the success of almost everything is in the follow up.

So, gentle email reminders or a chat on Facebook to see just how well she is doing is a great way to follow up on her commitments she gave to you on the day of the goal setting.

When the mum has completed and achieved her "Baby's New Carpet" goal, her confidence levels will be immense. Now she knows she can set her own goals and targets but most of all she knows she can achieve them too. Well done to you too, your navigation skills have shown her that she can now simply duplicate your efforts and do it with her team too. She has now became a Navigator of Dreams too.

My Nan says...

"Gail, you can lead a horse to water,

but you can't make it drink!"

But you can put salt in its oats

to make it thirsty!

My mum says...
"A chain is only as strong
as its weakest link"

If you can teach your team strong leadership skills from the beginning then they will follow and duplicate your teachings.

The best part of helping a team member to set and achieve goals is the completion of those goals. It is only then they realise that they are on a winning and extremely supportive team. From this experience with you, they will be ready to set a Bigger Goal. It should be a little harder to achieve and may take a little longer for them to reach it, but that's progress. It shows that your team leaders can begin to set their team's goals and incentives much the same as you have shown them. Therefore you and they are now "Thinking BIG" together.

So start by leading your team to success as a horse rider would lead his horse to water. Help them set a personal goal that is going to benefit them personally. Once the goal is set, then leave them to make their own decisions along the way (with your navigation and support, of course). But always keep at the forefront of your mind that you will never be able to force them to complete their goals. Unfortunately they may have become the stubborn horse and have decided not to complete their goals.

Always Remember

The horse that refuses to

drink the water

All Systems Go!

FINDING

SERVING

MAINTAINING

Your

CUSTOMERS

REPRESENTATIVES

TEAM LEADERS

Placing a system into your network is no easy feat. You have to consider a few things:

- What are your desired end results from your system?

- Is it a duplicatable system?

- What's in it for me?

If I start with the customers of the business I will show you a system I use to help find, serve and maintain them all. After all, everyone needs customers in their business so it's the ONLY place to start.

We first need to generate a customer and we have to gain her interest in our product and service. So as a business owner I expect you have customers of your own that you have generated already?

FINDING THE CUSTOMER

Before you begin the process, ask yourself a few questions:

"How do I find and generate customers for myself?"

Now write down your process of finding your own customers in great detail.

Next, write down your answers to these questions too:

Who do I speak to? - List the types of people you talked to - businesses, offices, shops, and mums at the school gates
What do they say? - Give simple feedback quotes of what the new team member can expect to hear

What did you reply? - Tell them about your different approaches towards different genders and age groups

Where did you go? - Places you visited - office blocks, housing estates, shops, hairdressers, day care, nursing homes and colleges perhaps?

Why did they become your customer? - Special offers, discounts, and gifts for 1st time buyers and recommendations maybe?

Now you are working on building a system within your own business, they need to be simple and easy to duplicate with your team. Keep these steps in mind when you create your systems:

They must be simple to:

- Show
- Share &
- Duplicate

Think about giving your team members the very best start in their business by offering a system for Finding, Serving and Maintaining a customer base.

Here are a few facts about customers:

Did you know that a customer makes the best representative and distributor for any product or service that you are providing? They utilise, wear, promote and talk about your product and service without being paid for it. Your customers are the only reason you are in business today. Without them, you would not be able to keep your business and network afloat.

Always remember that - **It's a fact!**

Now we have managed to simplify **finding** the customers the next part of the system is:

SERVING THE CUSTOMER

Again this is the part of the system where you simply write down your findings:

Contact- How do you keep in contact with your customer?

Email, text, or Facebook etc

Service – What is your <u>U P S</u>? Unique Personal Service?

- Do you visit at the same time every week on the same day?
- Do you have a One Stop Selling technique in place?
- Do your customers come to you for their products or service, or maybe you go to them?

Special offers - What offers do you provide for your loyal customers?

Do you run raffle prizes, have parties for them and their friends, maybe you provide coffee mornings to showcase your products and services?

Duplicate what we did in the "Finding a Customer" process and this will be the second part of your system. Write down your findings and we will move on to the third and final step.

The 3rd part of your system will include:

MAINTAINING THE CUSTOMER

This is the key to the success of you and your final working system.

What do you do? – Offer reliability, honesty, a high quality service, and your very own Unique Personal Service

How do you do it?

- With a precise and professional service
- A guaranteed money back service on all products
- Consistency

What's in it for you?

- CUSTOMERS = ORDERS
- ORDERS = SALES
- SALES = EARNINGS
- EARNINGS = ☺

Here are some examples of how a great system works in all kinds of businesses.

Ask yourself why you keep going back to your favourite coffee shop, restaurant or shoe shop?

The Coffee Shop

Is it because the coffee is great, the service is friendly and the consistency can always be found there? Maybe it's the fact they serve fast and very hot freshly made coffee too.

The Restaurant

Maybe it's because they offer great food at a reasonable price, with a fantastic atmosphere? Also, they play your favourite kind of music too which helps you relax and enjoy the experience even more.

The Shoe Shop

The owner and workers in the shoe shop are always polite and smile at the children when you arrive. They have a play corner for your children to play in whilst you try out the newest shoe styles too. Although the prices are higher than in most other shops, the service and products are more than worth the extra expense.

These types of systems are in place in every successful shop and business you enter. Ultimately this is what you are aiming to provide for your customers too. By implementing a system into your network or business will mean you will have an incredible business and simple system to duplicate.

You will be adding much more of a foundation for your team of new representatives and distributors to work with. Each and every single customer within your network and business will have a level of service that is second to none!

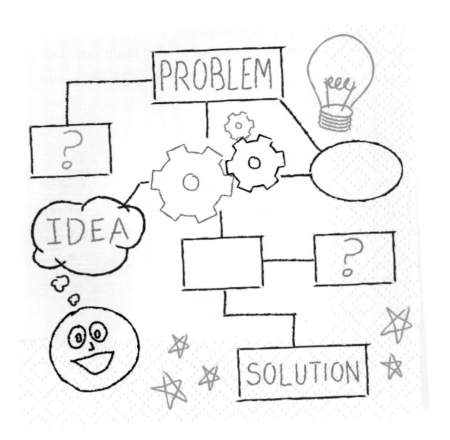

My mum says...
"Sharing your ideas is the
smart thing to do"

To re-cap on building a simple system, you need to remember to write things down. Remember to design the system in a simple format so that your team can then follow, train and duplicate it. Then simply watch your exponential growth within your business and network.

Before we finish on this subject I would like you to consider that you are a very unique individual and your systems need to be seen as that way too. Here is what you can do before you consider your business systems. Think about your most nearest and dearest friends or family members. Now choose 3 of them and set about asking them this question.

"If you had to describe me, how would you do it in just 3 words?"

I love this question, because most of the time, friends and family can surprise you with their answers. Often they don't say what you think they are going to say.

Your friends and family are really honest and trustworthy and they will be openly and brutally honest with you, if you allow them to be that is!

Whatever their answers are, these will become your unique selling qualities. These are what set you apart from the rest. Use them, mould them into your systems and create a business/vision that no one else can possibly recreate. I would like you to refer to page 62 in this book for a list of characteristics and traits you may find useful. Focus on what you are good at and I guarantee you will see a huge positive difference within your business, and in just a few days too.

"Honest"

"Quiet"

"Creative"

Create a Vision

To create a vision you must first create a picture in your mind's eye and then more importantly you must take action to make sure your vision becomes a reality. Creating the vision needs a little planning too, so we need to work out a few things about you, your team and business. Also when you are creating a vision and following it through you will need what we talked about earlier. Your belief system. Remember to draw a picture of what your vision is to encapsulate it in its entirety.

Allow your creativity and your beliefs to become the driving force behind your vision. To get you going, here are a few things you may want to ask yourself:

- Do you have an end of week, end of month and end of year goal?
- What systems do you have in place within your network and business?
- What does your team or business offer that's different to others?
- What are your personal and business desires and what are your team's dreams?

"I love it when my mummy picks me up from school every day"

Now I would like you to consider what your Values are?

I **value** my children's school run every day and the fact I can do it because of my business. I **value** my lifestyle and the ease of which I can change things and circumstances if I need to. It's a good idea to write down what you value the most about being a woman in business for yourself. Write it down on a sticky note and pop it on your computer or vision board.

When you begin working on your creative vision you need to start with a few basics in mind. How you manage your time will be crucial to your vision. I personally class time management as being one of the most important skill sets when making your vision a reality.

I simply use the urgent or important technique.

It's an **URGENT** use of my time to be at the school gates at 3pm every day to pick up Rosie. That task is in my diary every day as an urgent task that has to be done. I have no choice, and I value my time with Rosie on our walks home from school together.

My mum says...

"The washing can jolly well wait!"

It is **IMPORTANT** to get the washing on the line too, but it's not an urgent task for me as I could pop it into the tumble dryer later.

So imagine I get a call to recruit a new team member that afternoon; what do you think I will do with the washing?

Do I hang it out and put another load into the washing machine?

Or

Do I make an appointment to go recruit a new team member?

Planning your time wisely and into **URGENT** and **IMPORTANT** tasks is a great way to goal setting that works.

The way to create a vision will also include working with duplicatable systems, making sure you have them in place before you begin with your creative vision.

I have also discussed in the book how to become unique. Ask 3 friends or family members to describe just what type of person you are to them and work with your Unique Personal Qualities when creating your vision.

Also you will need to know exactly what it is your team and you desire from the business. What are your dreams and more importantly what are your team's dreams.

You need a clear picture of exactly what it is you want to achieve from your new and creative vision. Then last but certainly not least, what are your values within your business and network?

My Values

Belief and the power of belief within my team are the foundations of my business. To have every single team member take responsibilities and to be the very best they can be. When you believe in someone and show, act and behave so, then that individual will try their very best to prove you're right.

Respect helps us as a team to value one another's differences, to appreciate each person for their individual and unique qualities. Through respecting each and every individual amongst us we help bring out the full potential of each person.

Integrity should be the foundations of every business woman out there. Doing the right thing is always at the forefront of my business.

Trust means we want to live and work in an environment where communications are open - where the team feel happy and free to take risks, to share their points of view and to speak the truth as they see and feel it. I trust my team to do the right thing and I help them to understand my underlying reasoning and philosophy.

Humility simply means we're not always right. To become the student and know we don't have all the answers shows we are no less human than the people who work within our teams and networks. As their Team Leader, I am not afraid to ask them for their help.

By setting and observing the highest ethical standards we fulfil a duty of caring and sharing amongst our network. This applies not only to our customers, representatives and team leaders but within the communities we serve too.

Your unique vision should clearly represent you and your business ethics and values. Here is my vision for my business and its future.

My mum says...

"Help others open the doors to their
dreams,
And the doors to your dreams will be
opened too"

My Vision

For all customers I strive to provide a service to them that is of an outstanding value, high quality and of a personal nature. Each product we sell will be of the highest quality backed by a 100% money back guarantee and total customer satisfaction.

For all the representatives on my network, I intend to give them all the same opportunities to earn and learn whilst encouraging their entrepreneurial skills.

For my Team Leaders I work to provide training, leadership and innovative business ideas for them to take forward into their businesses and become the best they can be.

Throughout my business there will be full recognition and continued thanks and respect to all customers, representatives and team leaders. It is with the continued support and loyalty of these individuals and their contributions within my network that my business depends.

I will continually share with my network the rewards of growth and success and to incentivise them for their efforts.

_____

With this type of vision for my business and network I can wake every day knowing exactly what my business foundations are laid out on.

Here is a personal quote for my business Vision and Values.

> "Many people Talk
> but don't Do.
> Many people Think
> but don't Act.
> Many people Need
> but don't Believe."

I

DO

ACT

&

BELIEVE

Monte Carlo Winners 2010
Positioned in the Top 3 in the UK

Berlin Winners 2011
Positioned in the Top 3 in the UK

New York Winners 2009
Number 1 Achievers in the UK for
Team Growth in Sales & Recruitment

My mum says...

"When you work hard,

you deserve to play

hard as well"

Before I finish this chapter I would like to share something I found when working with my team of leaders, representatives and indeed from the friendly customers I have met over the years. I have found that whilst they are successful in their own way, each and every one are very different and unique in their own styles and personalities. With discovering this, I have not only had the pleasure of creating long lasting friendships with most of these wonderful women, but they have helped me build a very successful business too.

Where one woman may be a confident presenter and talker, the other could be an outstanding observer and listener. Another may be a go getter and launches into things like a bullet out of a gun, yet another will be calm, collective, quiet and subdued in their approach.

I can honestly tell you they have all been as effective and successful as each other.

Why? I believe it's because they are tapping into their own unique style, personality and vision within their business and network. They are using their own assets to become an outstanding Network Marketer, Direct Seller, Party Planner and business owner.

I have constantly been rethinking and rebuilding my work and business and I have constantly kept up with the times and the changes within it.

The difference in results that people produce simply boils down to the different actions they have taken. They have stood out from the crowd, gone in the direction they feel is best for them and achieved phenomenal success.

I think with all changes comes success. But to make changes effectively you need to take action. Not everyone likes to take action because it actually means they have to actually do something to achieve the desired results.

By always taking ACTION you will always guarantee results......

There are some simple steps you can take to get into action every single day. You can start with getting your pen and paper out and writing down 3 activities with which you will need to take action on. Here is an example of the type of action I need to take quite often within my business:

- How can I generate more sales?
- How can I grow my sales team?
- How can I use my money more effectively?

ACTIONS

More sales

Actively find more customers, put on your shoes and coat and take action by spending a morning putting postcards in shop windows. Maybe you could consider a leaflet drop. Go visit your loyal customers and talk to them, offer them free gifts and incentives for any recommendations they may have. To double and quadruple your efforts, ask your representatives and team leaders to join you.

Team Growth

Actively speak to your top 20% of representatives and distributors. Congratulate them on their success and ask if you can visit them with a gift. At the meeting, tell them how unique they are and how much they "Stand Out" from the rest of your team. Ask them if they would like to take their business forward. Tell them about the business opportunity you have to offer them.

Go to the search engines and begin using the following:

- Free ad sites
- Social networking sites
- Forums and chat rooms in your line of business
- Business directories

Simply make your presence known on the internet.

Money Management

Physically write down how much you are spending on a daily, weekly and monthly basis.

Now set them out individually.

For example:
Fuel costs = £40 a week
1000 leaflets cost = £20 a week

The way you could manage both these money matters could be by looking into your team and identifying whether you have a team member that lives just a few miles down the road from you. Then why not "Buddy Up" with them a couple of times a week. This way the cost of fuel is halved and you are both managing your money much more efficiently. You can do something similar with your leaflet budget too. I highly suspect the more leaflets you order the cheaper they become? Why not identify a team member that also purchases leaflets and add your stock numbers together to make one bulk order and divide the costs.

Personally I supply my entire team with prospecting cards (Recruitment Leaflets) because it's far cheaper than them going and buying them individually. I have 80,000 full coloured and glossy cards printed each time at an amazing price. They are generic cards for any one of my team leaders to use and personalise for themselves. They can use them for FREE - either they can collect them from my garage or they pay the postage and packaging and we send them out in the post the next day.

You can take a look at your advertising budget too. How much do you currently spend on advertising your business and the opportunities you have to offer? Is it worth splitting the cost and therefore the leads to help a fellow team member lower their costs and increase their team size?

Maybe you can talk to your team and talk about a syndicate where you all pool your advertising budgets and place a more professional advert in several papers?

These are all simple, easy and quick actions you can take that may help create solutions for your business today!

One of my last tips when you are creating your vision is to consider yours and indeed other people's feeling too. Feelings are a really important part of being the success you want to be. Feelings dictate to us whether we are happy, sad, angry, excited, tired...the list goes on. Within growing your wealth you need to identify these feelings at all times.

I make it a daily routine where I do or say two of the following things to strangers or friends alike:

- Send a card to the friend you haven't spoken to for a while
- Give to charity/take old clothes to the local second-hand shop
- Call a team member, tell her or him how proud you are of them and their achievements, and thank them for their work
- Be inspiring to others
- Say "Good Morning/Good Evening" to the next stranger you meet
- Send an email of gratitude to someone you admire

I guarantee by the end of today you will be feeling so good about yourself you will wonder why you hadn't done all this before.

> **"If it feels good then just do it, if you love the responses you're getting then keep doing it."**

Incorporating these feelings into your network and business life is essential to your success. I make a conscious effort to write my 1st email of the day with gratitude. It's a feeling that lasts all day!

As John Ruskin would say,

"Sunshine is delicious, rain is refreshing, wind braces us up, snow is exhilarating; there is really no such thing as bad weather, only different kinds of good weather."

When I read the quote from John Ruskin I thought to myself,

"One person's ideal, is another's greatest fear."

Keeping a positive outlook on change is a skill that needs mastering very early in any business. Whether you own a sweet shop, a hairdressers or a network marketing business. In all my years of experience "Change" is the one thing I can say will happen without a shadow of a doubt! So keep your mind open and positive towards change as it is inevitable in any business.

When creating your vision or taking actions within your business, remember your personal strengths and qualities. Use your greatest assets, your unique skill sets, and your ability to build a working system.

Have you ever thought back as to why you started your business, why did you open that shop? Or start that MLM, Network Marketing, Direct Selling or even Party Planning business?

I used to. But not anymore, now I remind myself that in my 1st month I sold just £50 worth of products and didn't earn much more than a fiver! When I became a leader I recruited 12 women in 3 weeks and didn't earn enough to take us to the cinema! But I kept going.

I believed that I could do it and I wasn't prepared to re-negotiate my goal, of working from home and owning my own business. I wanted my own home and my own life! Being able to have time off with my kids when I choose was always and still is at the forefront of my mind.

So, now when I remember my 1st few weeks in the world of independence, I have to pinch myself. From little ole me being a lonely old housewife, taking action, making a call and changing the way things were, I have now got everything I ever wished for and more. Me, my husband Brian and our 3 children have the freedom to make our own choices. Any mum or woman like me could do, have and make exactly the same choices too.

When I think back to the 1st lady that took a brochure from me in the playground, to the most recent team member I recruited, I am filled with such pride and passion. I have enjoyed every single moment of my business journey, and I continue to enjoy it to this very day. The fact that I have managed to help other children like my Rosie have their mummy's pick them up from school, fills me with pride and joy too. I know with sharing my ideas and successes with other women will help children have their mummy at home more often than not.

So if ever you are having a bad day, sit and reflect on what you are about to achieve and what you have already accomplished. Never ever look at what you haven't got or haven't achieved and don't dwell on what you don't have. Grab on to your dreams and goals with both hands. Complete your course and become a Navigator of your dreams like I have.

Take pride in what you do and what you have to offer. If you don't sell yourself then you will quickly sink into the background of the business you're in. Becoming a real life person and not just another "Network Marketer" is imperative for you to succeed.

If you don't create a system then your team will have nothing solid to duplicate and follow. I set myself a few goals when I became a part of my company. I believe because I completed those early goals it gave me the skills and courage to continue setting them and completing each and every one.

One of my tasks was to become an expert within the company and all it had to offer; I researched the company and its competitors and I have continued to do so to this very day. It has given me the ability to find and create great friendships within the company and within many other networks too.

To show my passion I also created a logo that resembles me and my team, and what we have to offer as both independent representatives and team leaders. I follow this through with every step I take in building my network.

Supplying AVON for YOU
Recruiting YOU for AVON
Giving YOU an opportunity

This brings me to the end of my book. I do hope you have enjoyed some of the tips and ideas I have covered with you and that you find the strength to grow your business as I do each and every day.

I look forward to standing side by side with you one day very soon, when we can link arms and shout out to the world

"My mummy has set you some homework. She say's if you complete it you can treat yourself to lots of huggles tonight with your little ones like me!"

Lists are Essential

- Build systems within your business and K.I.S.S (Keep It Simple Silly)
- Set high expectations for your business and your personal life
- Expect team members to duplicate what it is you do
- Create business goals for you and your team
- Be there always for guidance
- Lead from the front
- Master leadership and your entire life will be transformed

Worksheet 1

Unique Personal Service

Ask your friends and family,

"What 3 words best describe me?"

1.

2.

3.

"How can I use my unique qualities to make me stand out from the crowd?"

1.

2.

3.

The Belief Technique

Go to the mirror
Go on.... go to a mirror.... Look at yourself & say out loud

"I look great, I feel great, and I can do anything"

Worksheet 2

The Navigator of Dreams

Discover other team members' dreams and goals, and work only with the workers within your network.

Ask yourself "How can I monitor and motivate this team member?"

"What must I do with this team member that will serve them most effectively?"

Remember what your job is as a navigator and allow your team member to take control of their own destination.

Worksheet 3

Systems

FINDING

SERVING

MAINTAINING

When starting any new system keep in mind:

- K.I.S.S
- DUPLICATION

Worksheet 4

Gratitude Work and Life

- Today I will send a card to ....

- I will go give to charity/take old clothes to the local second-hand shop.

- Today I will call .... to tell her/him how proud I am of them and their achievements.

- Taking a book from the library about .... will inspire me today.

- I will say "Good Morning" to .... this morning.

- I will send an email of gratitude to .... today.

"Many people Talk
but don't Do.
Many people Think
but don't Act.
Many people Need
but don't Believe."

I
DO
ACT
&
BELIEVE

A Closing Message

Life can be tough but it's what you make it. You are the navigator of your dreams, so don't let others (fly your aeroplane) control your own business success.

Always remain focused and driven and never think anything is too BIG to achieve.

You are the only one person that can determine whether you fail or succeed in this business. Always keep in mind that there is no such thing as failure, just lessons to be learnt. You may not have achieved a specific goal but you definitely learnt how not to do it next time!

Remain positive; give all of yourself to those that are working towards the same goals.

From the day I started my networking business I knew it was for me. I wanted freedom to work when I wanted; I needed to be at home with my kids. I wanted a nice home, car, holidays and savings...

I also quickly realised that in no other business can you increase your earnings year on year without increasing your workload. I mean, who has a boss that doubles your income every few weeks, pats you on the back and says "Thanks, here is another salary increase for your efforts this month". I don't know any, do you?

My workload has not increased! But our time with our family however has. Our holidays have increased and so have our savings accounts. We have 2 cars on the drive and 2 homes. We enjoy weekends away when visiting family and even when we are working.

We incorporate our business into our personal life daily. Our kids think living with the business is a normal way of life. They also think it is normal to always have Mummy and/or Daddy taking them to and from school every day and to always have us both attend parents' evenings and sports days. They think it's a normal daily routine to wake up with the comfort of knowing if they are poorly and need us we are always there. We don't need to call in and "Ask for time off", we just take it.

As a mum in business this is what makes me the proudest. Being there as a parent and giving my children everything they could ever wish for.

From the bottom of my heart, I would like to thank my husband Brian for putting up with my constant excitement to life, business and this book. How he puts up with my new plans, ideas and findings. He has helped me provide for our family by being my constant.

I would like to thank my mum and dad. I am deeply proud of what you have both achieved these past few years with your own business. I told you, you are never too old and we all knew you could do it. Thanks.

A finishing thought

Do you want a little more?

Would you like some of your personal questions answered? Then feel free to visit me and my website at: www.gailreynolds.co.uk

I am there to support you. You are welcome to join our friendly forum too. Meet new people. Chat and discuss business issues and ideas with other women worldwide. Become part of the fastest growing women's network there is!

Because Pssst.....

MUM'S THE WORD